The Convicting Ministry of the Holy Spirit

The Convicting Ministry of the Holy Spirit

by
John MacArthur, Jr.

MOODY PRESS
CHICAGO

ISBN: 0-8024-5374-0

1 2 3 4 5 6 Printing/LC/Year 93 92 91 90 89

Contents

These Bible studies are taken from messages delivered by Pastor-Teacher John MacArthur, Jr., at Grace Community Church in Panorama City, California. The recorded messages themselves may be purchased as a series or individually. Please request the current price list by writing to:

WORD OF GRACE COMMUNICATIONS
P.O. Box 4000
Panorama City, CA 91412

Or call the following toll-free number:
1-800-55-GRACE

1

The Holy Spirit Testifies About Christ

Outline

Introduction
A. John 13—A Promise of Abiding Love
B. John 14—A Promise of the Coming Spirit
   1. A guarantee of Christ's return
   2. A guarantee of spiritual power
   3. A guarantee of answered prayer
   4. A guarantee of God's presence
C. John 15—A Promise of Increasing Opposition

Lesson
  I. The Christian Witness Is to the World
    A. Being Separate from the World's System
    B. Confronting the World's Sin
 II. The Christian Witness Is of the Son
    A. The Standards of Witnessing
      1. We must be exact
      2. We must exalt Christ
    B. A Survey of Witnessing
      1. In the Old Testament
      2. In the New Testament
III. The Christian Witness Is from the Father
    A. The Status of the Holy Spirit's Witness
    B. The Start of the Holy Spirit's Witness
    C. The Specifics of the Holy Spirit's Witness
      1. It's through the prophets of God
      2. It's through the works of Christ
      3. It's through the affirmation of the Father
IV. The Christian Witness Is Through the Spirit
    A. Acts 2:32-33
    B. Acts 5:29-32

7

Introduction

In John 15:26–16:15 Christ unfolds the Holy Spirit's ministries to His disciples. That section of Scripture is part of Christ's farewell address given on the night before His crucifixion. It was a night of great sorrow for the disciples. Therefore, beginning in John 13:31 Christ comforts them.

A. John 13—A Promise of Abiding Love

Christ comforted the disciples by giving them a graphic demonstration of His love—He washed their feet. Through Christ's example, the disciples learned that they should love others through humble service.

B. John 14—A Promise of the Coming Spirit

Christ then told the disciples that He needed to return to His Father. They should rejoice and not be sorrowful, He said, for He would send a comforter—the Holy Spirit. The Holy Spirit would enable the disciples to do "greater works" than Christ did when He was with them (v. 12). The presence of the Holy Spirit is the key to the fulfillment of Christ's promises. In John 16:14 Jesus says, "He [the Holy Spirit] shall glorify me; for he shall receive of mine, and shall show it unto you." The Holy Spirit's ministry is to take the promises of Christ and make them operative in the life of every Christian.

1. A guarantee of Christ's return

In John 14:3 Jesus says, "If I go and prepare a place for you, I will come again." Jesus promised to return, and we know from 2 Corinthians 5 that the Holy Spirit is the guarantee of that promise: "We know that if our earthly house of this tabernacle were dissolved, we have a building of God, an house not made with hands, eternal in the heavens. . . . Now he that hath wrought us for

8

the very same thing is God, who also hath given unto us the earnest of the Spirit" (vv. 1, 5).

The Greek word translated "earnest" (*arrabōn*) means "down payment" or "security." In modern Greek the word has been used to refer to an engagement ring. The Holy Spirit is our guarantee that Christ will come again and take us with Him to heaven.

2. A guarantee of spiritual power

We have already seen that Christ promised the disciples that they would have the ability to do mighty works (John 14:12). Acts 1:8 tells us where the power came from: "Ye shall receive power, after the Holy Spirit is come upon you." Ephesians 3:20 says that we as Christians will be "able to do exceedingly abundantly above all that we ask or think, according to the power that worketh in us." The Holy Spirit makes Christ's promise of power a reality.

3. A guarantee of answered prayer

In John 14:13-14 Jesus says, "Whatever ye shall ask in my name, that will I do, that the Father may be glorified in the Son. If ye shall ask anything in my name, I will do it." Christ promised the disciples that He would hear and answer their prayers when they asked in His name. Romans 8 says that the Holy Spirit "maketh intercession for the saints according to the will of God" (v. 27). Thus, the Holy Spirit is the key to prayer also.

4. A guarantee of God's presence

In John 14:18-23 Christ promises the disciples that He and God the Father will come and abide with them. Their presence in a believer is realized by the indwelling Holy Spirit.

C. John 15—A Promise of Increasing Opposition

After giving many positive promises, Christ gave the disciples a negative promise that I believe is applicable to every follower of Christ. He warned the disciples, "Because ye

9

are not of the world, but I have chosen you out of the world, therefore the world hateth you" (v. 19). The system of the world is opposed to Christ and therefore is opposed to those who follow Him. The world hates Christians because Christ lives in them. Being the object of the world's hatred is a good indication that a person is God's child.

Lesson

John 15:26-27 says, "When the Comforter is come, whom I will send unto you from the Father, even the Spirit of truth, who proceedeth from the Father, he shall testify of me; and ye also shall bear witness, because ye have been with me from the beginning." The Holy Spirit communicates truth to a hostile world through the conviction of sin and the witness of Christ. When we are energized by the Holy Spirit we can boldly face the hostile world with the gospel of Jesus Christ.

"Testify" (v. 26) and "witness" (v. 27) are legal terms. The apostle John used the imagery of a law court in this passage, with the judge representing the world, the prisoner representing Jesus Christ, and the prosecutor representing Satan. The counsel for the defense represents the Holy Spirit, and the witnesses represent Christians, who are briefed by the defending counsel so that their testimony will be potent.

A Supernatural Confrontation

Acts 17:6 says that first-century believers "turned the world upside down." The context of the verse illustrates why. Verse 4 says, "Some of them believed, and consorted with Paul and Silas; and of the devout Greeks a great multitude, and of the chief women not a few." On the other hand, verse 5 says, "The Jews who believed not, moved with envy, took unto them certain vile fellows of the baser sort, and gathered a company, and set all the city in an uproar, and assaulted the house of Jason, and sought to bring them out to the people." When confronted with the claims of Christ, some believed them, some ignored them, and some reacted with hostility. It's no different today. Likewise, our need to rely upon the power of the Holy Spirit remains the same.

In John 15:26-27 Christ gives us the pattern for an effective witness to a hostile world.

I. THE CHRISTIAN WITNESS IS TO THE WORLD

Verses 26-27 are embedded in a section of Scripture detailing the hostility of the world. Verse 18 talks about the world, verses 19 through 25 address the world, and the first few verses of chapter 16 deal with the hateful world. The context before and after our passage speaks of the world's hatred. The world is the object of our witness. Some people give testimony of Christ only to other Christians. They've never confronted the world. Yet Jesus said, "Go ye into all the world, and preach the gospel" (Mark 16:15). Obviously Jesus meant for us to confront the world with the good news of salvation.

A. Being Separate from the World's System

To confront the world effectively we must be separated from its system. We can't confront the world if we are absorbed in it. James said, "Whosoever . . . will be a friend of the world is the enemy of God" (4:4). And John said, "If any man love the world, the love of the Father is not in him" (1 John 2:15).

Until the day it passes away (1 John 2:17), the world will remain the enemy of Jesus Christ because it is controlled by Satan (1 John 5:19). The evil system of the world has been designed by Satan to destroy Christ. That has been Satan's goal from the time of his fall, and it will continue to be his goal until he is cast into the bottomless pit (Rev. 20:10). Satan manipulates the world through sin in an attempt to achieve his objective, which is why believers are to hate the world. That doesn't mean we are not to love the people in the world. It means that we are called to confront the world with its sin.

B. Confronting the World's Sin

Even though we must be separated from a world controlled by Satan, we must not withdraw from it completely. Rather, we must confront the world as the disciples did. Such confrontation will bring us persecution, but we must

11

not retreat. We should face persecution bravely, counting it an honor to share in the sufferings of Christ. If the world hated Christ, it will also hate us. The world is set against Christianity.

II. THE CHRISTIAN WITNESS IS OF THE SON

Jesus Christ is the content of the Christian witness. We must not accommodate our message to the world like so many others have done. Rather, we must proclaim the offense of the cross, which is the Person and work of Christ.

A. The Standards of Witnessing

1. We must be exact

The apostle Paul said, "There are some that trouble you, and would pervert the gospel of Christ. But though we, or an angel from heaven, preach any other gospel unto you than that which we have preached unto you, let him be accursed. As we said before, so say I now again, If any man preach any other gospel unto you than that ye have received, let him be accursed" (Gal. 1:7-9). We must present Christ accurately.

2. We must exalt Christ

God desires that we confront the world with a testimony about Christ—not ourselves. In the right context it is proper to share with someone what Christ has done in our lives—just as Paul did. But our testimony must be given in such a way that it focuses attention on Christ. People must know who Christ is; who we are is secondary.

B. A Survey of Witnessing

The testimony of the true church throughout history has been Jesus Christ. John said the purpose of the book of Revelation was to bear "witness of the word of God, and of the testimony of Jesus Christ" (1:2). In chapter 12 he says that all believers are characterized by the "testimony of Jesus Christ" (v. 17). In chapter 19 he adds, "The testimony of Jesus is the spirit of prophecy" (v. 10).

1. In the Old Testament

Old Testament writers focused on the coming Christ, although at times they did not fully understand their own prophecies. First Peter 1 says, "Of which salvation the prophets have inquired and searched diligently, who prophesied of the grace that should come unto you, searching what, or what manner of time the Spirit of Christ who was in them did signify, when he testified beforehand the sufferings of Christ, and the glory that should follow" (vv. 10-11). Clearly Christ was the central theme of their prophecies.

2. In the New Testament

Jesus said, "Ye shall receive power, after the Holy Spirit is come upon you; and ye shall be witnesses unto me both in Jerusalem, and in all Judaea, and in Samaria, and unto the uttermost part of the earth" (Acts 1:8). In the New Testament Christ instructs the disciples to give witness about Him.

If our witnessing is truly empowered by the Holy Spirit, Christ will be the subject of our testimony. Christ says in John 16:14, "He [the Holy Spirit] shall glorify me."

III. THE CHRISTIAN WITNESS IS FROM THE FATHER

Two times in John 15:26 Christ indicates that the Holy Spirit comes from the Father: "When the Comforter is come, whom I will send unto you *from the Father,* even the Spirit of truth, who *proceedeth from the Father,* he shall testify of me" (emphasis added). The witness of the Holy Spirit originated with the Father.

The Mystery of the Trinity

John 15:26 implicitly teaches us about the Trinity. The Son is speaking, the Spirit is being sent, and the Father is planning the mission. But the exact nature of the relationship among the members of the Trinity remains a mystery. For example, in John 14:16 Christ says, "I will pray the Father, and he shall give you another Comforter." Verse 26 says, "The Comforter, who is the Holy Spirit, whom the

Father will send in my name." In the first verse it seems as though Christ intends to send the Spirit, and in the second verse it seems as though the Father intends to send Him. Many times the inter-working of the Trinity is beyond our understanding. I cannot comprehend the Trinity. But I do know from Scripture that in a sense both the Son and the Father were responsible in sending the Holy Spirit.

A desire to specify the Trinity beyond what we know from the Word of God will lead to serious theological error. The heresy called Modalistic Monarchianism is one such instance. This theory asserts that God exists in only one Person or mode at any given time. First God was the Father, then God was the Son, and last God was the Holy Spirit. However, Scripture does not allow for such an understanding of God. In fact, in John 15:26 the members of the Trinity are interacting with one another. So the Father, Son, and Holy Spirit must exist in separate Persons at the same time, yet somehow remain one (Deut. 6:4).

A. The Status of the Holy Spirit's Witness

Jesus emphasized that the Spirit would be sent from the Father to the disciples. The disciples knew that Christ came from the Father and would be going back to the Father. Christ also emphasized that the Holy Spirit is equal to Himself. In John 14:16 Christ says, "I will pray the Father, and he shall give you another Comforter." The Greek word translated "another" (*allos*) frequently refers to another of the same kind. The Holy Spirit is fully God. Therefore, since the Holy Spirit is God and has been with God from all eternity, He is a qualified witness.

B. The Start of the Holy Spirit's Witness

When did the Holy Spirit come as a witness of Jesus Christ? Christ promised the disciples, "Ye shall receive power, after the Holy Spirit is come upon you; and ye shall be witnesses unto me" (Acts 1:8). Jesus' promise was fulfilled on the Day of Pentecost (Acts 2). The Holy Spirit came from the Father at Pentecost to witness to the Son. The Spirit witnesses to the Son by indwelling believers.

14

C. The Specifics of the Holy Spirit's Witness

1. It's through the prophets of God

Jesus says in John 5:39, "Search the scriptures; for in them ye think ye have eternal life; and they are they which testify of me." "Scriptures" refer to the books of the Old Testament. Throughout the Old Testament the Father was testifying of Jesus Christ. In fact, Luke 24:27 says that "beginning at Moses and all the prophets, [Christ] expounded unto [two of His disciples], in all the scriptures, the things concerning himself."

2. It's through the works of Christ

Jesus said, "I have greater witness than that of John [the Baptist]; for the works which the Father hath given me to finish, the same works that I do, bear witness of me, that the Father hath sent me" (John 5:36). Through the works that Jesus did, the Father was giving testimony. Again Christ says, "I told you, and ye believed not; the works that I do in my Father's name, they bear witness of me" (John 10:25). The works that Jesus did were the Father's testimony.

3. It's through the affirmation of the Father

Several times God the Father gave testimony to Jesus by direct statement. In Matthew 3:17 He says, "This is my beloved Son."

The passion of the Father is to bring men the testimony of Jesus. If we are to bear fruitful witness to the world—to proclaim the testimony of Jesus—we must use the Bible, for that is where we read of the Father's testimony to the Son. And certainly we cannot enhance the testimony of the Father to the Son. The Word of God, then, is the key to our witness.

IV. THE CHRISTIAN WITNESS IS THROUGH THE SPIRIT

The Father's testimony is given to the world through the Holy Spirit.

15

A. Acts 2:32-33—"This Jesus hath God raised up, whereof we all are witnesses. Therefore, being by the right hand of God exalted, and having received from the Father the promise of the Holy Spirit, he hath shed forth this, which ye now see and hear." The coming of the Holy Spirit on the Day of Pentecost made witnessing possible.

B. Acts 5:29-32—"Peter and the other apostles answered, and said, We ought to obey God rather than men. The God of our fathers raised up Jesus, whom ye slew and hanged on a tree. Him hath God exalted with his right hand to be a Prince and a Savior, to give repentance to Israel, and forgiveness of sins. And we are his witnesses of these things; and so is also the Holy Spirit, whom God hath given to them that obey him." The apostles saw their witness in connection with the Holy Spirit. And the Holy Spirit's witness is always concerned with presenting Jesus Christ.

C. Acts 4:31—"When they had prayed, the place was shaken where they were assembled together; and they were all filled with the Holy Spirit, and they spoke the word of God with boldness." The natural result of being filled with the Spirit is witnessing. Notice that the Holy Spirit is called the Spirit of truth. The Holy Spirit never tells anything but the truth; He is the perfect witness. He not only leads people to truth but also is truth in essence. In John 16:14-15 Jesus says, "He [the Holy Spirit] shall glorify me; for he shall receive of mine, and shall show it unto you. All things that the Father hath are mine; therefore said I, that he shall take of mine, and shall show it unto you." The Spirit dispenses the truth of Christ to every believer.

D. 1 John 5:6—"This is he that came by water and blood, even Jesus Christ; not by water only, but by water and blood. And it is the Spirit that beareth witness, because the Spirit is truth." Since the Spirit is truth, He must bear witness to Christ, because Christ is truth (John 14:6).

All Filled Up with No Place to Go?

There's no such thing as a Spirit-filled Christian who never witnesses, for the Spirit's ministry is to testify about Christ. Spirit-

16

filled people confront the world because that's what the Spirit directs them to do. Hebrews 2:4 says of the apostles that God bore "them witness, both with signs and wonders, and with diverse miracles and gifts of the Holy Spirit." The apostles were given supernatural gifts by the Holy Spirit so they could dispense the gospel.

In Romans 15:19 Paul says, "Through mighty signs and wonders, by the power of the Spirit of God, so that from Jerusalem, and round about unto Illyricum, I have fully preached the gospel of Christ." The filling of the Holy Spirit enabled Paul to preach the gospel of Christ. And the Holy Spirit continues to empower God's people to tell of God's Son.

V. THE CHRISTIAN WITNESS IS IN THE BELIEVER

The Christian witness is of the Son, from the Father through the Spirit, and in the believer. The believer is the last link in the chain of witnesses. Unlike Jesus, the Holy Spirit has not chosen to physically manifest Himself in a human body. Rather, the Holy Spirit embodies the church—the Body of Christ now present on earth. Ephesians 2:22 says of the church, "Ye . . . are built together for an habitation of God." God wants to witness to the world through us. We are the last link in God's plan to reach the world.

The Essence of Our Testimony

In John 15:27 Christ gives an important qualification for being a witness: "Ye have been with me from the beginning." What is it that makes a witness legitimate? A witness has to have seen what happened to be credible. You can't go into a court and be a witness unless you saw what happened. For example, I once saw an attempted murder. That qualified me as a witness to that incident, and I went to court and gave my testimony. The only person who can give a testimony is someone who has experienced something. That takes our testimony of Jesus out of a cold, factual realm into the warmth of personal experience. But the testimony itself is not our personal experience. That's the *motive* for our testimony. Our personal experience may elucidate our testimony, but our testimony itself has to do with Jesus Christ and His work on the cross.

17

We are the final step in the witnessing process. How tragic it would be if the witness of Christ broke down because of us. Romans 10:14-15, 17 says, "How, then, shall they call on him in whom they have not believed? And how shall they believe in him of whom they have not heard? And how shall they hear without a preacher? And how shall they preach, except they be sent? As it is written, How beautiful are the feet of them that preach the gospel of peace, and bring glad tidings of good things! So, then, faith cometh by hearing, and hearing by the word of God." In His sovereignty God has designed Christians to be the channels that the Holy Spirit uses to give witness of Christ.

Focusing on the Facts

1. What is the context of Christ's discussion on the Holy Spirit's ministries in John 15:26–16:15 (see p. 8)?
2. The Holy Spirit's ministry is to take the _____ of _____ and make them _____ in the life of every Christian (see p. 8).
3. Identify the "power that worketh in us" (Eph. 3:20; see p. 9).
4. Why does Christ promise to answer our prayers (John 14:13-14; see p. 9)?
5. Give one condition of answered prayer (John 14:13-14; see p. 9).
6. What negative promise did Christ give to His disciples (John 15:19; see pp. 9-10)?
7. Explain the legal imagery of John 15:26-27 (see p. 10).
8. Who is the object of the Christian's witness according to the context of our passage (see p. 11)?
9. Why is the world an enemy of God (James 4:4; 1 John 2:15-17; see p. 11)?
10. What judgment awaits those who pervert the gospel (Gal. 1:7-9; see p. 12)?
11. Did Old Testament prophets know about and speak of Christ? Explain (1 Pet. 1:10-11; see p. 13).
.12. How does John 15:26-27 contradict heresies about the Trinity such as Modalistic Monarchianism (see p. 14)?
13. How does the Greek term translated "another" in John 14:16 support the deity of the Holy Spirit (see p. 14)?

14. When was Christ's promise recorded in Acts 1:8 fulfilled (Acts 2; see p. 14)?

15. What must we take in hand when we confront the world with the testimony of Jesus Christ (see p. 15)?

16. What is the relationship between being Spirit-filled and giving testimony about Christ (see pp. 16-17)?

17. What is an important qualification of being a witness (John 15:27; see p. 17)?

Pondering the Principles

1. It has been said that the finger that points out the path we must walk is connected to the hand that upholds us. Christ promises to be with us as we pursue godly living in a hostile world. In Matthew 28:20 He comforts us, saying, "I am with you always, even unto the end of the age." Have you retreated from the task of confronting the world because of opposition? Or perhaps a lack of understanding the Holy Spirit's ministries is the cause. If you are a believer, you can be assured that the Comforter lives within you. He desires to use your life to testify of Christ. But spiritual power is directly dependent upon time spent with Christ. Jesus told the disciples, "Ye . . . shall bear witness, *because ye have been with me from the beginning*" (John 15:27, emphasis added). Sometimes the simplest principles are the ones we overlook. We need to spend time exposing our hearts to the Lord through prayer and the study of His Word on a regular basis. Commit yourself to a specific time of prayer and Bible study, and be sure to stick to it.

2. This lesson has brought into focus our responsibility to testify of Christ. To accomplish that, God has given His Spirit to us. One responsibility we do not have, however, is to save people from their sins. The results of the gospel must be left in the hands of God. Therefore, the question is, Are you faithful to witness? not, Are you winning people to Christ?

3. Man's greatest need is forgiveness. Christianity is based on forgiveness. However, forgiveness presupposes a debt—one caused by sin—that must be canceled. Thus a clear presentation of the gospel must include the fact that sin has destroyed man's

19

relationship with God. A faithful witness must confront sin. The next time you explain the gospel to someone, make sure he knows he's lost before you tell him the good news that he can be saved. That's the only way he will be able to appreciate the value of salvation.

2
The Holy Spirit Convicts the World—Part 1

Outline

Introduction

Lesson
 I. The Killing of the Disciples by the World (vv. 1-4)
   A. The Promise Given (v. 1)
     1. The preparation
     2. The principle
   B. The Persecution Described (vv. 2-4a)
     1. Its certainty (vv. 2a, 4a)
     2. Its nature (v. 2b)
     3. Its motive (v. 2c)
     4. Its cause (v. 3)
   C. The Pronouncement Delayed (v. 4b)
     1. In degree
     2. In direction
 II. The Comforting of the Disciples by the Lord (vv. 5-7)
   A. The Selfishness of the Disciples (vv. 5-6)
     1. Established
     2. Extracted
   B. The Selflessness of Christ (v. 7)

Introduction

The gospel of John presents Jesus as God in human flesh. As I mentioned in the previous lesson, chapter 16 is a record of Christ's last night with His disciples. The crucifixion would change Christ's present relationship with His disciples. Physically, Christ would no longer walk beside them. In a sense the disciples would have to face the world alone. Christ understood the difficulties that the disciples would face and comforted them. The disciples would face a world in rebellion against God. After Christ returned to the Father, the world would vent its hatred of Christ on His representatives. The hostility and hatred of the world is the focus of this lesson.

In John 15 we saw that the Spirit confronts the world with the testimony of Christ by indwelling God's children. In many ways the first eleven verses of chapter 16 parallel the last two verses of chapter 15. In chapter 15 Jesus is detailing the hatred of the world and presenting the work of the Holy Spirit in confronting the world. But in chapter 16 Christ specifies how the Spirit confronts the world—He convicts people of sin. Chapter 15 ends with the testifying ministry of the Spirit, and chapter 16 opens with the convicting ministry of the Spirit. By bearing testimony to Christ and convicting people of sin, the Spirit seeks to turn the hostile hearts of people away from rebelling against God and toward receiving Jesus Christ as Savior and Lord.

Lesson

I. THE KILLING OF THE DISCIPLES BY THE WORLD (vv. 1-4)

A. The Promise Given (v. 1)

"These things have I spoken unto you, that ye should not be offended."

"These things" refers to what Christ spoke of in John 15:18-25—the hatred of the world. Jesus told His disciples about the coming hatred of the world because He didn't want them to be surprised when they encountered it. Christ wanted the disciples to be prepared through His warning.

The Greek verb translated "offended" (skandalizō) is transliterated into English as "scandalize." The noun (Gk., skandalon) was used to refer to the stick that held up the trap into which an animal was lured by bait. The animal would be captured when it grabbed the bait, which was tied to the stick. The skandalon was the trigger that pulled the trap

22

down. Jesus used the analogy of a trap to warn the disciples to be alert. He didn't want them to stumble into a trap set by the world. Jesus taught them the full meaning of discipleship—the pain as well as the joy.

1. The preparation

The disciples failed many times despite the warnings they received. Their failure would probably have been greater, however, had they not been warned. What if they hadn't known about the hatred of the world? What if all they knew were the promises of love, joy, peace, answered prayer, the power to do greater works than Christ, and the promise of a Comforter who would energize and empower them? If that were all they knew, they would have been totally unprepared for persecution. They would have faltered when the world's hatred was directed at them. Jesus wanted them to understand that the opposition they would face was part of God's plan. Therefore, He tenderly and compassionately prepared the disciples.

2. The principle

The disciples didn't have to fail. In fact, Christ gave them everything they needed to prevent failure. Nevertheless, Christ knew that they would one day betray Him. From the divine perspective, they had been given all they needed to stand firm. But at the same time God did not violate their freedom of choice. The principle of human responsibility means that man can choose whether or not he will apply the truth and the promises of God. Man has the freedom to reject God's help. When the hour of persecution came, the disciples rejected what they knew to be true and ran away out of fear.

As Christians today, we aren't much different from the disciples. We have about the same knowledge and wisdom God gave to them. Although Colossians 2:10 says that we are complete in Christ, when we are faced with a problem we are often afraid and doubt our relationship with God. Many times we stumble and fall into sin. It's not that we don't have what we need from God; often it is simply that we reject the resources God has given us. Instead of calling on the supernatural resources God has made available to us, we fall back on our humanness. The power to overcome the world is not in ourselves but in Christ.

B. The Persecution Described (vv. 2-4a)

1. Its certainty (vv. 2a, 4a)

Christ added detail to what He said in chapter 15 by telling the disciples what kind of persecution they would face. Verse 2 says, "They shall put you out of the synagogues . . . whosoever killeth you will think that he doeth God service." Before his conversion, the apostle Paul was a partial fulfillment of that verse. In Acts 26:9-11 Paul says, "I verily thought within myself, that I ought to do many things contrary to the name of Jesus of Nazareth, which thing I also did in Jerusalem; and many of the saints did I shut up in prison, having received authority from the chief priests. And when they were put to death, I gave my voice against them. And I punished them often in every synagogue, and compelled them to blaspheme; and being exceedingly mad against them, I persecuted them even unto foreign cities." Paul pursued and killed Christians, thinking he was performing a service to God.

Persecution of Christians still goes on today. Although you may not be persecuted to the point of death in America, if you live a godly life you will suffer persecution. The world doesn't regard Jesus any better now than it did in the first century. And a man who stands up and defends the name of Jesus Christ is going to attract the world's hatred. In verse 4 Jesus says, "These things have I told you, that when the time shall come, ye may remember that I told you of them." Christ told the disciples about the coming persecution so that when it came they would remember that He told them, and their faith would be strengthened. One of the greatest ways to strengthen faith is to see fulfilled prophecy, which I believe is the greatest proof of the divine authorship of the Bible. History verifies the Word of God.

Christ says essentially the same thing in John 14: "Now I have told you before it come to pass, that, when it is come to pass, ye might believe" (v. 29). "Believe" is another word for "faith." To build up their faith when it happened, Jesus told the disciples beforehand that He would go away and come again.

2. Its nature (v. 2b)

Christ said that the disciples would be "put out of the synagogues" (Gk., *aposunagōgous*, "unsynagogued"). To the Jewish people at that time, being a member of the synagogue was essential. All social, economic, and religious life was connected with the synagogue. A person cast out of the synagogue was considered a moral outlaw—worse than a pagan Gentile.

In John 9 the parents of the healed blind man "feared the Jews [the religious leaders]; for the Jews had agreed already that, if any man did confess that he [Jesus] was Christ, he should be put out of the synagogue" (v. 22). These parents didn't want to be ostracized from Jewish life. The disciples were no different in this respect, and yet Christ knew that they would be cut off from their people. Certain Jewish leaders would focus their hatred for Him on His followers. Eventually all the disciples would be cast out of the synagogue, and some would be killed.

3. Its motive (v. 2c)

The depth of the world's sin is seen in the colossal mistake it made of thinking it was serving God by killing Christ and His followers. Throughout history, the persecutors of Christians and others have been under the delusion that they were ministers of God. The early church's persecution by Rome, the Crusades, and the Spanish Inquisition were all done in the name of God.

The Greek word translated "service" (*latreuō*) is used for the service of priests at the altar. It's the standard word for religious service given to God. The people who persecuted the Christians believed that they were carrying out worship when they slaughtered people who named the name of Christ.

4. Its cause (v. 3)

Why do people persecute Christians and believe that they're doing God a favor? What kind of a God do they worship? I believe that they worship a god of their own creation—a fictitious deity. Verse 3 says, "These things will they do unto you, because they have not known the Father, nor me." The problem is that they don't know God. Jesus said to the religious leaders, "If ye had known me, ye should have known my Father also" (John 8:19).

The problem has always been the same: people worship a god who doesn't exist. They slaughtered Christ and His disciples as though they were sacrifices to a deity. What an abominable mistake! Jesus said they do that because they're ignorant—they don't know God. The sad part is that it's a willful ignorance (Rom. 1:18-21). People willfully reject *the* God and construct *a* god of their own.

Jesus promised the disciples that persecution against them would come in the name of God. The best way Satan can discredit God is to do in the name of God things that are obviously atrocities. That's why Satan focuses his efforts on religious activities.

C. The Pronouncement Delayed (v. 4*b*)

"These things I said not unto you at the beginning, because I was with you."

1. In degree

Christ knew that it would be difficult for His disciples to bear the news of persecution, so rather than telling them at the beginning of His ministry, He waited until His death was near. In the early stages of Christ's ministry it would not have been profitable for Him to tell the disciples of the persecution they were to experience, but now, at this late hour, they needed to know of it.

26

Nevertheless, Christ broached the subject earlier in His ministry. In Matthew 5:10-12 and 10:16-39 Christ tells the disciples to expect abuse from the world. In fact, He told them that they would be reviled and persecuted. Yet He did not tell them the depth of the persecution—that the whole world would be set against them. He waited until the last night of His earthly life to warn them fully about the world's hatred.

2. In direction

Christ said the reason He did not tell the disciples about the full fury of the world's persecution was that He was with them (John 16:4-7). Christ absorbed the brunt of the world's attack when He walked upon the earth. Throughout the gospels we find that the world didn't attack the disciples. Even when the disciples did something the religious leaders didn't like, the religious leaders went to Jesus. Christ had been the focus of the world's attacks—but that would soon change. Christ would no longer be in the world physically, so the world would have to direct its attack against the ones closest to Him—His disciples. Similarly, Satan is set against Christ, and if he can't get at Christ, he will attack His disciples.

Objects of Satan's Wrath During the Tribulation

A powerful illustration of Satan's attack against those who belong to Christ is the Tribulation, which will be the greatest outpouring of Satan's wrath. In Revelation 12:9 Satan is represented as a dragon. Verse 4 says, "His tail drew the third part of the stars of heaven and did cast them to the earth; and the dragon stood before the woman who was ready to be delivered, to devour her child as soon as it was born." The woman in this verse represents Israel, and the child represents Christ. During the thirty-three years Christ lived on earth, Satan tried to devour Him by such means as Herod's decree, the temptation in the wilderness, and the cross. But he was unsuccessful.

Yet Satan didn't allow those failures to stop him. Since Satan couldn't devour the child, he tried to devour the woman (Israel)

27

who brought forth the child: "When the dragon saw that he was cast unto the earth, he persecuted the woman who brought forth the child" (v. 13). Not content to merely persecute the nation of Israel, Satan "went to make war with the remnant of her seed, who keep the commandments of God, and have the testimony of Jesus Christ" (v. 17). Satan will attack everyone who has anything to do with Jesus Christ.

Jesus told His disciples that the world was going to persecute them. And the world is still persecuting those who belong to Christ. Satan "like a roaring lion walketh about, seeking whom he may devour" (1 Pet. 5:8). Peter gave that warning to believers, not unbelievers. Paul says in Ephesians 6:11-12, "Put on the whole armor of God, that ye may be able to stand against the wiles of the devil. For we wrestle not against flesh and blood, but against principalities, against powers, against the rulers of the darkness of this world, against spiritual wickedness in high places." We're in a battle with Satan, who is using the world against us to propagate his deadly doctrines.

II. THE COMFORTING OF THE DISCIPLES BY THE LORD (vv. 5-7)

A. The Selfishness of the Disciples (vv. 5-6)

"Now I go my way to him that sent me; and none of you asketh me, Where goest thou? But because I have said these things unto you, sorrow hath filled your heart."

Christ was grieved because He saw the selfishness of His disciples. Apparently their only concern was how Christ's going away would affect them. They weren't concerned about how Christ would be affected by His return to the Father. Instead they were mumbling about their own problems. In John 14:28 Jesus says, "If ye loved me, ye would rejoice, because I said, I go unto the Father." Rather than rejoicing over Christ's return to the Father, the disciples appeared disinterested.

28

1. Established

Nevertheless there is an apparent contradiction: In John 13:36 Peter asks, "Lord, where goest thou?" And in 14:5 Thomas says, "Lord, we know not where thou goest; and how can we know the way?" Why then did Jesus say, "None of you asketh me, Where goest thou?" (John 16:5)?

Apparently when the disciples asked, "Lord, where are you going?" they did so because they wanted to know if they were going with Him. Peter said, "Lord, why cannot I follow thee now?" (John 13:37). Peter wanted to go with Christ even if he had to die. But when Jesus tells them in chapter 16 that they will be staying behind, no one bothers to ask where He is going because it doesn't involve them. When the disciples thought they were going with Christ, they were eager to find out where they were going. But when Christ said that He was leaving and that they would have to face the hostility of the world, the disciples were concerned about themselves, not Christ.

In chapter 13 the disciples are not questioning Jesus to find out what going away meant to Jesus; they are asking because they thought it involved them. They were selfish. They saw only their own sorrow. Yet we are not much different. We are most concerned about the things that affect our own lives. Some people never learn to step outside their private world and look at things from Christ's perspective, and in so doing, praise Him.

2. Extracted

But the disciples didn't remain self-centered. Luke 24:50-53 says that the resurrected Christ "led them out as far as to Bethany; and he lifted up his hands and blessed them. And it came to pass, while he blessed them, he was parted from them, and carried up into heaven. And they worshiped him, and returned to Jerusalem with great joy; and were continually in the temple, praising and blessing God." Jesus was gone, yet

His followers continued to praise Him. They were changed because their faith had been strengthened by Christ's death and resurrection.

B. The Selflessness of Christ (v. 7)

"I tell you the truth: It is expedient for you that I go away; for if I go not away, the Comforter will not come unto you; but if I depart, I will send him unto you."

Rather than rebuking the disciples for their selfishness, Christ gave them comfort. He reassured them that His death would bring about good. Through His death would come forgiveness of sins and reconciliation with God. Through His resurrection Christ would conquer death on behalf of all people. And after Christ left the earth, the Holy Spirit would come to indwell His disciples, giving them the power to realize the promises of the Father. So it was better for Christ to leave.

Going and Coming

Jesus said, "If I go not away, the Comforter will not come unto you" (John 16:7). The Holy Spirit's comforting ministry would not begin before Christ returned to the Father. The reason is found in verse 14: "He [the Holy Spirit] shall glorify me; for he shall receive of mine, and shall show it unto you." The Holy Spirit could not display the redemptive work of Christ until it was accomplished. Thus the Spirit could not come until the Son accomplished His task. Did Jesus finish His work? In John 17:4 He says, "I have finished the work thou gavest me to do." In turn, God responded by giving the Spirit to dwell within believers.

Jesus Christ has long since returned to the Father, but the Holy Spirit continues to indwell us. It's true that the world hates Christians; but in spite of all its hostility and hatred, Jesus said we have a Comforter who will strengthen, empower, and energize us to give testimony of Christ and convict people of sin. What a tremendous promise! In their own strength the disciples couldn't confront the world, but energized by the Holy Spirit they turned the world upside down. And so can we!

30

1. "These things" in John 16:1 refers to what (see p. 22)?
2. Explain the meaning of the Greek word translated "offended" in John 16:1 (see p. 22).
3. Explain how before his conversion the apostle Paul partially fulfilled John 16:2 (Acts 26:9-11; see p. 24).
4. What is another word for faith (John 14:29; see p. 25)?
5. Why did the Jewish people fear being put out of the synagogue (John 16:2; see p. 25)?
6. What does the term translated "service" mean in John 16:2 (see pp. 25-26)?
7. How does right knowledge affect worship (John 16:3; see p. 26)?
8. Why did Christ wait until the end of His ministry to tell His disciples about the depth of persecution they would face (John 16:4; see pp. 26-27)?
9. Who is the dragon in Revelation 12:9 (see p. 27)?
10. Identify the child and woman in Revelation 12:13 (see p. 28).
11. Explain why there is no contradiction between John 16:5 and John 13:36 (see pp. 28-29).
12. How did Christ's resurrection affect the disciples (Luke 24:50-53; see pp. 29-30)?

Pondering the Principles

1. When we think of God's loving care for His children, we usually turn to passages such as Psalm 23 and Isaiah 40. Although we may not think of John 16:1-7 as such a passage, in many ways it tells us of God's concern and involvement in our lives. Some claim that God is not personal in nature or that He doesn't care about mankind. In contrast, how is God's care for His children evident in this passage?

2. We tend to forget God's many provisions when we have experienced an extended period of ease (Deut. 8:11-18). That is one reason trials are to be counted as a blessing from God (James 1:2-5). Realizing that we tend to forget past divine provision and that we need encouragement to confront a hostile world, in the Old Testament God instructed His children to establish memorials. Those memorials served as reminders of God's gracious

dealing with His children in the past (e.g., Josh. 4:9). They strengthened the faith of believers as they faced new difficulties. Think of ways that you and your family could establish personal memorials so that you don't forget the good things God has done for you.

3
The Holy Spirit Convicts
the World—Part 2

Outline

Review
I. The Killing of the Disciples by the World (vv. 1-4)
II. The Comforting of the Disciples by the Lord (vv. 5-7)

Lesson
III. The Convicting of the World by the Spirit (vv. 8-11)
    A. The Barrier to Conviction
        1. Man is defiled
        2. Man is hostile
    B. The Object of Conviction (v. 8)
        1. Man's heart condemned
        2. Man's heart convinced
    C. The Instruments of Conviction (vv. 9-11)
        1. "Sin" (v. 9)
        2. "Righteousness" (v. 10)
        3. "Judgment" (v. 11)

Review

John's gospel presents the full deity and humanity of Jesus Christ.
Chapter 16 is a special occasion, for it is the night before the crucifixion. Christ's farewell discourse with His disciples begins in
chapter 13. In that chapter He talks with them about His love. In
chapter 14 and the first part of chapter 15 Jesus gives the disciples
marvelous promises that will be fulfilled because He is going away.

In chapter 15, however, Christ warns them that the world will try to kill them because of its hatred for Christ. Persecution is inevitable, because a true disciple opposes the system of the world, which is under Satan's control. Yet Jesus comforted His disciples by saying, "In the world ye shall have tribulation: but be of good cheer; I have overcome the world" (John 16:33).

I. THE KILLING OF THE DISCIPLES BY THE WORLD (vv. 1-4)

In John 16 Jesus says, "These things have I spoken unto you, that ye should not be offended. They shall put you out of the synagogues; yea, the time cometh, that whosoever killeth you will think that he doeth God service" (vv. 1-2). The disciples were not to be surprised that people would try to kill them in the name of religion. History verifies that that is exactly what happened. All kinds of atrocities take place in the name of religion. False religion always persecutes those who speak God's truth. Jesus said, "These things will they do unto you, because they have not known the Father, nor me" (v. 3). It's frightening to realize that people who claim to be serving God don't even know Him! Commitment to external religion is no guarantee that that person is a true believer. A person may go to church, carry a Bible, and read his prayer book, and yet have no personal relationship with God. Religious people do not necessarily know God. Some are trapped and blinded by a system, having no idea who God or Christ is.

In verse 4 Christ says, "These things have I told you, that when the time shall come, ye may remember that I told you of them. And these things I said not unto you at the beginning, because I was with you." When Christ was with the disciples, He was the object of the world's attacks. But after He returned to the Father, the disciples became the focus of its hatred.

II. THE COMFORTING OF THE DISCIPLES BY THE LORD (vv. 5-7)

After Christ warned the disciples, He comforted them. In verses 5-6 He says, "Now I go my way to him that sent me; and none of you asketh me, Where goest thou? But because I have said these things unto you, sorrow hath filled your heart." He pointed out that the disciples feared only for themselves instead of caring about His destiny.

Christ continued, "Nevertheless, I tell you the truth: It is expedient for you that I go away; for if I go not away, the Comforter will not come unto you; but if I depart, I will send him unto you" (v. 7). Christ knew that it was best for Him to return to the Father, for the Holy Spirit would then come to indwell the disciples and other believers.

Lesson

III. THE CONVICTING OF THE WORLD BY THE SPIRIT (vv. 8-11)

A. The Barrier to Conviction

The convicting ministry of the Holy Spirit deals with the problem of sin.

1. Man is defiled

The Bible says that every man is a sinner. Paul remarked, "As it is written, There is none righteous, no, not one" (Rom. 3:10; Ps. 14:3). Everyone in the world has rebelled against God. Christ alone is perfect. Man is sinful not only in behavior but also by birth. As the offspring of our rebellious first parents, Adam and Eve, we all are born sinners. People don't understand God, so they run from Him.

Although some people believe that they are good, Scripture says, "They are all gone out of the way, they are together become unprofitable; there is none that doeth good, no, not one" (Rom. 3:12). Evil people usually do not consider what they do to be evil. Rather, most believe that they are doing good. Paul described them well when he said, "Their throat is an open sepulcher; with their tongues they have used deceit; the poison of asps is under their lips; whose mouth is full of cursing and bitterness. Their feet are swift to shed blood; destruction and misery are in their ways; and the way of peace have they not known. There is no fear of God before their eyes" (vv. 13-18).

35

People are in rebellion against God. When you are born into the world, you enter under the world's system, which is controlled by Satan—the original rebel against God.

2. Man is hostile

Because the world is under Satan's control, it hates Christ. Furthermore, men and women who don't know Christ hate those who know Him, because Christians act as a living condemnation of them. Sinfulness hates righteousness, and imperfection hates perfection. Yet though God is opposed to unrighteousness, He loves the world.

The Holy Spirit's ministry is to break down the resistance people have to Christ and bring them into fellowship with God. For that to occur, Christ first needed to break the power of sin, which holds men in rebellion against God. Sin separates mankind from God.

B. The Object of Conviction (v. 8)

"When he [the Holy Spirit] is come, he will reprove the world of sin, and of righteousness, and of judgment."

John 15:26 says that the Holy Spirit will testify to the world about Christ. But now we see another aspect of the Spirit's ministry: bringing conviction of sin. He reveals man's sin, which compels man to seek God's mercy through the work of Christ on the cross. Therefore, we know that no man will come to Christ until he recognizes his sinfulness.

1. Man's heart condemned

The key to understanding verse 8 is the Greek word translated "reprove" (*elegchō*). It has two meanings: "condemn" and "convince." In the first sense it speaks of convicting with a view toward judgment or sentencing. It's a courtroom term a judge would use to declare guilt and pronounce judgment. The Holy Spirit reproves people by declaring them guilty. People merit that condemnation because they have rejected Jesus Christ. Although the Holy Spirit makes the declaration,

He is not the One who carries out the condemnation. That responsibility belongs to the King of kings and Lord of lords—the Lord Jesus Christ Himself (John 5:27-29).

2. Man's heart convinced

Elegchō can also mean "convince." The Holy Spirit condemns people, and He convinces them that they need Jesus Christ. The convincing ministry of the Holy Spirit precedes the condemning ministry; in other words, if we do not respond to His convincing truths we will be condemned.

We are convinced by the Holy Spirit when we have a subjective realization of guilt. But why does the Holy Spirit want us to grasp the full realization of our sinfulness? Because an awareness of our sinfulness will bring us to an understanding of our need for a Savior.

Painful Love

Pain is often beneficial. Without pain we wouldn't know when we were hurt and thus would be unable to prevent our deaths. Similarly, the Holy Spirit reveals our sins and needs. Through an awareness of our needs we are driven to Christ as the fulfillment of those needs. His ministry of convincing is an act of love. Without it man would continue on a course to hell.

The Spirit's task is to bring people to Jesus Christ by exposing their sin. I've seen that ministry at work in people who are burdened by an overwhelming sense of sin. That indicates to me that they are ready to receive Christ. It's exciting to meet people who are painfully aware of their sinfulness, because self-righteous people don't see themselves as needy.

C. The Instruments of Conviction (vv. 9-11)

"Of sin, because they believe not on me; of righteousness, because I go to my Father, and ye see me no more; of judgment, because the prince of this world is judged."

The Holy Spirit uses three things to convict people: sin, righteousness, and judgment.

1. "Sin" (v. 9)

"Of sin, because they believe not on me."

In the final judgment a person goes either to heaven or to hell depending on whether or not he believes in Jesus Christ. The Spirit tries to convince people not to reject Christ, for rejecting Christ leads to condemnation.

Note that "sin" is singular in verse 9. For the most part the Holy Spirit doesn't convict unbelievers of all the sins they've ever committed. Rather, He concentrates on convicting them of the sin of rejecting Jesus Christ, which is consistent with the Spirit's ministry of revealing Christ. John 3:18 says, "He that believeth on him [Christ] is not condemned; but he that believeth not is condemned already, because he hath not believed in the name of the only begotten Son of God." Condemnation is the result of unbelief. In John 5:40 Jesus says, "Ye will not come to me, that ye might have life." Man's problem is the sin of not believing in Christ, not the individual sins he has committed. In John 8:24 Jesus says, "I said, therefore, unto you, that ye shall die in your sins; for if ye believe not that I am he, ye shall die in your sins."

If you stand before the Great White Throne on Judgment Day, it will not be simply because of the sins of your daily life. Rather it will be because you rejected Jesus Christ. The issue is whether or not you believe in Christ as He revealed Himself. Mark 16:16 says, "He that believeth and is baptized shall be saved; but he that believeth not shall be damned." God knows every sin we commit, but the issue isn't one of keeping a record of every sin that we have ever committed, for condemnation is a matter of sin—not sins. The issue is your belief in Christ.

In Christ's day thousands died by crucifixion. What makes the death of one man who was declared to be a criminal so significant? Why does the death of Christ on the cross grip men's hearts so that they cannot ignore Jesus? The reason is the convicting ministry of the Holy Spirit.

2. "Righteousness" (v. 10)

"Of righteousness, because I go to my Father, and ye see me no more."

The world has no adequate sense of righteousness. In 1 Corinthians 4:3-5 Paul says, "I don't even judge myself. My conscience is clear, but that does not make me innocent. It is the Lord who judges me. . . . He will bring to light what is hidden in darkness and will expose the motives of men's hearts" (NIV*). We will condemn ourselves if we measure ourselves by ourselves. We must follow the one true standard of righteousness—Jesus Christ. The Holy Spirit wants to show us the righteousness of Christ so we'll understand our sinfulness.

The righteousness of Christ is best demonstrated by the fact that God accepted Christ back into His presence. That's what the phrase "because I go to my Father and ye see me no more" speaks of. On the cross God laid sin upon Christ. Through His obedience, however, Christ was raised in righteousness. And His righteousness was proved because the Father accepted Him back.

a) Habakkuk 1:13—"Thou [God] art of purer eyes than to behold evil, and canst not look on iniquity." The fact that Jesus entered into the presence of the Father shows that God considered Him to be righteous.

b) Philippians 2:9-11—"God also hath highly exalted him, and given him a name which is above every name, that at the name of Jesus every knee should bow, of things in heaven, and things in earth, and things under the earth, and that every tongue should confess that Jesus Christ is Lord, to the glory of God, the Father." The way God treated Christ showed that Christ is righteous.

*New International Version.

39

c) 1 John 3:10—"Whosoever doeth not righteousness is not of God." Entrance into the presence of God is dependent upon righteousness. We enter heaven because Christ's righteousness has been imputed to us. When you put your faith in Christ and receive Him as your Savior and Lord, His righteousness becomes yours, and you can enter into the presence of God.

d) Acts 10:35—"In every nation he that feareth him [God], and worketh righteousness, is accepted with him." Acceptance with God is based on righteousness.

e) Romans 4:5—"To him that worketh not, but believeth on him that justifieth the ungodly, his faith is counted for righteousness." You are made righteous only when you've put your faith in Jesus Christ, accepting His death on your behalf and repenting of your sin.

f) Romans 3:26—"To declare, I say, at this time his [God's] righteousness, that he might be just, and the justifier of him who believeth in Jesus." Salvation isn't an issue of how good or how evil you are; it's a matter of believing in Jesus Christ.

One ministry of the Holy Spirit is to convince people that Jesus is righteous. The Spirit uses the Bible and the godly lives of Christians to accomplish that. In Philippians 3:7-9 Paul expresses the heart of a redeemed man: "What things were gain to me, those I counted lost for Christ. Yea doubtless, and I count all things but loss for the excellency of the knowledge of Christ Jesus, my Lord; for whom I have suffered the loss of all things, and do count them but refuse, that I may win Christ, and be found in him, not having mine own righteousness, which is of the law, but that which is through the faith of Christ, the righteousness which is of God by faith."

3. "Judgment" (v. 11)

"Of judgment, because the prince of this world is judged."

40

The prince of this world, Satan, was judged on the cross. Though the death of Jesus Christ at first looked like Satan's greatest victory, it proved to be Satan's death blow because Jesus rose from the grave. Hebrews 2:14-15 says that Christ became man "that through death he might destroy him that had the power of death, that is, the devil, and deliver them who, through fear of death, were all their lifetime subject to bondage."

Colossians 2:15 says that Christ triumphed over Satan and his hosts. Revelation 20:1-3 says that in the end Christ will cast Satan in a pit and bind him for a thousand years. Then He will cast him into the lake of fire where he will remain forever. Satan is a defeated foe. God has judged Satan and will judge the world as well. If Jesus Christ can judge the greatest sinner in the universe—Satan—He can and will judge all unbelievers. God crushed Satan at Calvary, and that judgment is the guarantee that others will be judged.

The Holy Spirit reveals the folly of rejecting Christ. The Spirit shows you that Christ is the true standard of righteousness. He does that because He loves you and wants you to admit your sin and come to Jesus. Acts 24:24-25 tells us that "when [Roman governor] Felix came with his wife, Drusilla, who was a Jewess, he sent for Paul, and heard him concerning the faith in Christ. And as he reasoned of righteousness, self-control, and judgment to come, Felix trembled, and answered, Go thy way for this time; when I have a convenient season, I will call for thee." The Bible doesn't record that Felix ever had a "convenient season." Paul was used by the Holy Spirit to show Felix sin, righteousness, and judgment, but Felix asked him to go away. It is a serious error to ignore the convicting ministry of the Holy Spirit.

Focusing of the Facts

1. False religion always persecutes those who speak _____ _____ (John 16:3; see p. 34).
2. How did Christ's return to the Father alter the focus of the world's persecution (see p. 34)?

3. How does Romans 3:10 affect our understanding of the need for the Holy Spirit's convicting ministry (see p. 35)?
4. What will be the issue of the final judgment (see p. 37)?
5. Why is it significant that John 16:9 uses the singular rather than the plural of the word *sin* (see p. 38)?
6. What one sin can lead to eternal condemnation (John 3:18; see p. 38)?
7. How does Christ's return to His Father demonstrate our Lord's righteousness (John 16:10; see p. 39)?
8. On what basis are Christians allowed entrance into heaven (see p. 40)?
9. When will God bring final judgment upon Satan? What will be his ultimate end (see p. 41)?
10. What was Felix's response to the righteousness of Christ (Acts 24:24-25; see p. 41)?

Pondering the Principles

1. Most of us have had the experience of getting lost. At first you may have refused to acknowledge that you really did not know where you were, thus postponing your search for help. After all, why ask for directions when you know where you are, where you're going, and how to get there? It is similar in the spiritual realm. Individual men and women must be confronted with their sin before they will seek redemption through faith in the work of Christ on the cross. The subject of sin is not popular, because it makes all of us uncomfortable. But that is exactly what the Holy Spirit wants to do—disrupt our deceptive comfort. The smugness of the Pharisees is particularly instructive in this regard. The righteousness they thought they saw in themselves was a barrier to their salvation. Review the Scriptures, noting how Christ confronted religious people who were lost (e.g., Matt. 23). Then ask God for the wisdom to confront family members or friends who have been blinded by their religion.

2. A person is condemned when he has rejected Jesus Christ. Therefore we must focus our presentation of the gospel on the Person and work of Christ. It is easy to be sidetracked into discussing the specific sins an unbeliever has or has not committed and thereby fail to emphasize that it's the sin of unbelief that condemns a person to hell. There are three elements to a biblical presentation of the gospel: who Christ is, what Christ did, and

how that applies to all mankind (cf. 1 Cor. 15:1-4). It is essential that we identify and articulate the essential elements of the gospel.

3. Proverbs 29:1 warns, "A man who remains stiff-necked after many rebukes will suddenly be destroyed—without remedy" (NIV). There is a genuine danger of ending up like those "whose consciences have been seared as with a hot iron" (1 Tim. 4:2, NIV). As we have seen, one of the Holy Spirit's functions is to convict men and women of their sin. His main way of doing that is through your conscience. If the Holy Spirit is trying to tell you something, don't put Him off. Examine what is troubling you in the light of Scripture, and immediately make any necessary changes so that your conscience might remain usable.

4
The Spirit of Truth

Outline

Introduction
A. Adjustment by Liberal Theologians
B. Addition by Religious Groups
C. Authentication by God
  1. The Bible claims it is written by God
    a) Its unity
    b) Its historical accuracy
    c) Its extent of knowledge
    d) Its scientific accuracy
    e) Its paradoxes
  2. Christ claims it is written by God

Lesson
 I. The Reason for Revelation
 II. The Person of Revelation
   A. Inspiration of Truth
     1. The Old Testament was inspired by the Holy Spirit
     2. The New Testament was inspired by the Holy Spirit
   B. Incapacity for Error
III. The Purpose of Revelation
IV. The Pattern of Revelation
   A. The Holy Spirit Does Not Deviate from the Past (13*b*)
     1. In harmony with the Trinity
     2. In harmony with the Bible
   B. The Holy Spirit Details the Future (13*c*)
   C. The Holy Spirit Discloses the Glory of Christ (vv. 14-15)

Introduction

In John 16:12-15 Christ promises the disciples that the Holy Spirit will guide them in understanding the Word of God. Because the Bible is the Word of God, it is trustworthy, authoritative, and sufficient.

A. Adjustment by Liberal Theologians

Some theologians neither fully accept nor fully reject the authority of the Bible. Rather, they claim that it *contains* the Word of God and assume that it is the task of scholars to identify which texts are or are not God's Word. Other theologians believe that by personal experience the Bible *becomes* the Word of God to a particular individual at a particular time. The common fallacy evident in all liberal theology is placing man as judge over Scripture to determine what is truly God's Word.

B. Addition by Religious Groups

Many cults and religious groups add to the Word of God. The Church of Jesus Christ of Latter-Day Saints (Mormons) believes that the writings of Joseph Smith and others are just as inspired as the Bible. Members of Christian Science add the writings of Mary Baker Eddy to the Word of God. Jehovah's Witnesses depend on the writings of Charles Taze Russell and Joseph Franklin Rutherford to interpret the Scriptures. One mark of all cults is that they recognize an extrabiblical authority.

C. Authentication by God

Regardless of what others claim, however, the Word of God is final and complete. Although there are commentaries on the Bible, no new revelation is being given by God. The apostle John said, "If any man shall add unto these things, God shall add unto him the plagues that are written in this book" (Rev. 22:18). Clearly that verse affirms that revelation has ceased—and not only in the book of Revelation. Jude 3 speaks of "the faith that was once for all entrusted to the saints" (NIV).

There are many witnesses that attest the Bible is the inspired Word of God.

1. The Bible claims it is written by God

   a) Its unity

   Sixty-six different books were written over fifteen hundred years by at least forty authors. Yet there are no irreconcilable contradictions in Scripture, and a unified theme pervades Scripture.

   b) Its historical accuracy

   There are no historical errors in the Bible. Previously questioned biblical facts, such as the destruction of Jericho, have been vindicated by archaeological discoveries.

   c) Its extent of knowledge

   The Bible reveals facts that no one could determine on his own. Details about God, heaven, hell, and future events—all beyond man's ability to determine—are recorded in the Bible.

   d) Its scientific accuracy

   In the seventeenth century William Harvey discovered how the circulatory system keeps a person alive. But Genesis, the first book in the Bible, says that life is in the blood (9:4). Through the years people have concocted fantastic explanations of the earth's position and shape. But Job, the oldest book in the Bible, says that God "hangeth the earth upon nothing" (26:7). Isaiah 40:22 tells us that the earth is a sphere.

   e) Its paradoxes

   A final way the Word of God affirms itself is by recording facts that are too unpleasant for any human author to invent on his own. For instance, if man wrote the Bible, it is unlikely that he would have given the disparaging view of mankind that Scripture does. Man's sin and judgment would have been eliminated, as would have been the many paradoxes in the Bible. The presence of such difficulties attests to the supernatural character of Scripture.

2. Christ claims it is written by God

Jesus Christ is the supreme witness to the inspiration of Scripture. He believed that inspiration extended to the very words of Scripture. In fact, some of His lessons depend on a specific verb tense (e.g., Matt. 22:23-33) or the repetition of a specific word (e.g., Matt. 22:41-46; cf. Ps. 110:1). In Matthew 5:17-18 Christ says, "Think not that I am come to destroy the law, or the prophets; I am not come to destroy, but to fulfill. For verily I say unto you, Till heaven and earth pass, one jot or one tittle shall in no way pass from the law, till all be fulfilled." Indeed, Christ said that "scripture cannot be broken" (John 10:35).

There are at least three possible explanations for Christ's saying what He did about the Bible. One might say that He was aware of errors but didn't want to tell us. Yet that explanation is inconsistent with His character as it is revealed in Scripture. It would mean He deliberately hid the truth from us and thus was not trustworthy. Second, one might say that He was unaware of errors. But if He were unaware of errors, He couldn't have been God, and thus the explanation contradicts Scripture. Third, one might say that there are no errors in Scripture. That explanation agrees with Psalm 119:89, which says, "Forever, O Lord, thy word is settled in heaven."

Lesson

Christ's authentication of the Bible brings us to our text, which teaches that the Holy Spirit is the key to understanding inspiration. The Holy Spirit moved upon the minds of the authors to write the very words of God, yet He did not violate their individuality. Christ promised that the Holy Spirit would indwell believers, giving them the power to bear witness about Christ. As believers bear witness, the Spirit convicts unbelievers of their sin. In John 16:12-15 Christ adds another element of the Spirit's ministry: He guides people into truth through the ministry of inspiration.

I. THE REASON FOR REVELATION (v. 12)

"I have yet many things to say unto you, but ye cannot bear them now."

Jesus knew that at this time the disciples could not bear all He had to say to them because of their great sorrow. They had been with Christ three short years and were limited in their understanding of spiritual matters. They were anticipating the establishment of God's kingdom on earth and were confused when they heard Christ speak of His death. They loved the Lord and wanted to be with Him—the thought of His death distressed them.

Christ knew His disciples were immature and fearful. So rather than rebuking them, He tenderly loved them by letting them know He understood their weaknesses and ignorance. The disciples were faced with the difficult task of correctly interpreting the cross, the resurrection, and the ascension before these events took place. In Luke 18 Christ foretells His death, saying to the disciples, "Behold, we go up to Jerusalem, and all things that are written by the prophets concerning the Son of man shall be accomplished. For he shall be delivered unto the Gentiles, and shall be mocked, and spitefully treated, and spit on; and they shall scourge him, and put him to death. And the third day he shall rise again. And they understood none of these things; and this saying was hidden from them, neither knew they the things which were spoken" (vv. 31-34). Jesus realized that all those truths wouldn't come into focus until the Holy Spirit took up residency within the disciples and taught them.

In verse 12 Christ says He has "many things" to share with them. I don't believe that His statement refers to new revelation; rather it seems to indicate Christ's intention to clarify revelation He had already given them. The basics He had imparted to them needed to be amplified. In fact, that's exactly what the New Testament epistles do: amplify and apply the Person and work of Christ.

49

II. THE PERSON OF REVELATION (v. 13a)

"Nevertheless, when he, the Spirit of truth, is come, he will guide you into all truth."

The Holy Spirit would be the agent communicating the revealed will of God. Since Christ would no longer be with His disciples, the Spirit would continue His ministry to God's children. The Holy Spirit would be their helper (Gk., *parakletos*). He would not only activate Christ's promises but also would guide men into truth by revealing God to them. The Holy Spirit would guide men into all the truth necessary to salvation and godliness. He would have a unique ministry to the disciples by enabling them to write the New Testament.

A. Inspiration of Truth

1. The Old Testament was inspired by the Holy Spirit

It is important to note, however, that the Spirit's ministry of inspiration is not new. The Old Testament was given by inspiration of the Spirit. In Acts 1:16 Peter says, "Men and brethren, this scripture must needs have been fulfilled, which the Holy Spirit, by the mouth of David, spoke." The Holy Spirit wrote the Old Testament by speaking through men. Peter also told his readers that "no prophecy of the scripture is of any private interpretation. For the prophecy came not at any time by the will of man, but holy men of God spoke as they were moved by the Holy Spirit" (2 Pet. 1:20-21). The Old Testament was written by men who were inspired by the Holy Spirit. The Holy Spirit is the author of the Old Testament.

Hebrews 10:15-16 says, "The Holy Spirit also is a witness to us; for after he had said before, This is the covenant that I will make with them after those days, saith the Lord: I will put my laws into their hearts, and in their minds will I write them" (cf. Jer. 31:31-34). The covenant given in Jeremiah is attributed to the Holy Spirit. Many times the Old Testament is said to be the words of God given through men inspired by the Holy Spirit.

2. The New Testament was inspired by the Holy Spirit

First Corinthians 2 says, "As it is written, Eye hath not seen, nor ear heard, neither have entered into the heart of man, the things which God hath prepared for them that love him. But God hath revealed them unto us by his Spirit; for the Spirit searcheth all things, yea, the deep things of God. . . . Which things also we speak, not in the words which man's wisdom teacheth, but which the Holy Spirit teacheth, comparing spiritual things with spiritual" (vv. 9-10, 13; cf. Isa. 64:4). Paul declared the teaching of the Holy Spirit.

B. Incapacity for Error

John 16:13 says that the Holy Spirit is "the Spirit of truth." Everything the Spirit says is true. As God, He has no capacity for falsehood. He cannot lie. Therefore, there are no errors in the Bible, for He produced it. If there is an error in the Word of God, 2 Peter 1:20 is not true.

When the authors of the New Testament wrote the gospels and the epistles, they were inspired by the Holy Spirit. He used the very words of the authors in communicating what God wanted to say. That's what is known as verbal, plenary inspiration. *Verbal* inspiration means that every word of Scripture—not merely the thoughts or ideas—is inspired. *Plenary* inspiration means that every part of Scripture is inspired.

We cannot add anything to Scripture. Furthermore, we don't need to, for God insured that Scripture contains all we need to know to live in a manner that is pleasing to Him. The Bible is complete. A believer is "thoroughly furnished unto all good works" (2 Tim. 3:17). Sixteenth-century French theologian John Calvin said, "Whoever thinks that anything ought to be added to [the apostle's] doctrine, as if it were imperfect and incomplete, not only accuses the apostles of dishonesty, but blasphemes against the Spirit. . . . nothing can be added to them without terrible injustice to the Spirit" (*Calvin's Commentaries: The Gospel According to St. John*, translated by T. H. L. Parker [Grand Rapids: Eerdmans, 1961], p. 119).

The primary application of John 16:13 is to the disciples and the other New Testament writers. But it also applies to every believer. Rather than inspiring us to write Scripture, the Holy Spirit illuminates the Word so that we can understand the Bible. John said, "Ye have an unction from the Holy One, and ye know all things. . . . The anointing which ye have received of him abideth in you, and ye need not that any man teach you; but as the same anointing teacheth you of all things, and is truth, and is no lie, and even as it hath taught you, ye shall abide in him" (1 John 2:20, 27). The Holy Spirit continues to instruct us out of the Word.

III. THE PURPOSE OF REVELATION

Christ promised that the Holy Spirit would come and guide us into all truth. I believe He is a guide to every Christian, leading each one to spiritual maturity. Therefore the purpose of revelation is to guide us to the truth. That is accomplished when we understand God's Word and it changes our lives. The Holy Spirit ministers to us so that we will continue to grow to be like Christ.

IV. THE PATTERN OF REVELATION (v. 13b-15)

A. The Holy Spirit Does Not Deviate from the Past (13b)

"He [the Holy Spirit] shall not speak of himself, but whatever he shall hear, that shall he speak."

1. In harmony with the Trinity

The Holy Spirit would not give a different message. Rather, His ministry would be consistent with Christ's. This was an important promise for the disciples to understand, because they didn't know the Spirit in the way they knew the Father and the Son. Therefore, Christ told them that they could be confident that the Spirit would not speak independently of God and Himself. There is perfect harmony in the ministry of the Trinity.

52

2. In harmony with the Bible

The Holy Spirit's ministry is also consistent with the Word of God. In my ministry I have had to deal with people who have missed that truth. For instance, one couple was having sexual relations outside of marriage, yet they asserted that the Holy Spirit led them to do it (cf. 1 Cor. 6:18). Others have claimed that they were led by the Spirit to get a divorce (cf. Mal. 2:16). Another professing believer told me the Holy Spirit directed him not to read his Bible or attend church (cf. 1 Pet. 2:2; Heb. 10:24-25). Others have said that the Spirit told them not to serve or give money to the church (cf. 1 Pet. 4:10-12; 1 Cor. 16:1-2). However, we can be sure that the Holy Spirit does not lead people to do something that contradicts the Word of God. The mind of God and the leading of the Holy Spirit are always in agreement. One sure way to test whether you are being led by the Spirit is to examine the Bible.

B. The Holy Spirit Details the Future (13c)

"He [the Holy Spirit] will show you things to come."

Christ promised that the Spirit would unveil future events to the disciples. That includes the rapture (1 Thess. 4:13-18; Rev. 3:10), the Tribulation (2 Thess. 2:3-4; Rev. 4-19), the kingdom of God (Rev. 12:10; 20:4), the eternal state (Rev. 21:1–22:5), and heaven (Rev. 4-22). In fact, on the Day of Pentecost the Holy Spirit prophesied about the last days through Peter (Acts 2:16-21; cf. Joel 2:28-32). In addition, the Spirit reveals things to come in Acts 20:23 and 21:4. Revelation 1:1 says, "The Revelation of Jesus Christ, which God gave unto him, to show unto his servants things which must shortly come to pass." Beginning with the church age, God revealed things that were to take place in the future. The pattern of the Spirit as seen throughout the New Testament is to reveal the future.

Revealer of the Past, Present, and Future

The Spirit also reveals the past. John 14:26 says, "He shall teach you all things, and bring all things to your remembrance." Furthermore, the Spirit teaches in the present. Christ said of the Holy Spirit, "He shall testify of me" (John 15:26). He testifies to the present glory of Jesus. Then in John 16:13 we read that He shows us of things to come. The Holy Spirit reveals "all truth" (John 16:13)—past, present, and future.

C. The Holy Spirit Discloses the Glory of Christ (vv. 14-15)

"He shall glorify me; for he shall receive of mine, and shall show it unto you. All things that the Father hath are mine; therefore said I, that he shall take of mine, and shall show it unto you."

Jesus wanted the disciples to remember that He has intimate fellowship with the Father. The Holy Spirit reveals Christ, and Christ reveals the Father. The intended purpose of the Spirit's ministry is to make Christ and the Father known. In 1 Corinthians 12:3 Paul says, "I give you to understand that no man speaking by the Spirit of God calleth Jesus accursed; and that no man can say that Jesus is the Lord, but by the Holy Spirit." Knowledge of Christ comes through the Holy Spirit.

The Spirit puts Christ on display. He reveals a person, not a system. Christ wants us to be like Him. Second Corinthians 3:18 says, "We all, with unveiled face beholding as in a mirror the glory of the Lord, are changed into the same image . . . by the Spirit of the Lord." And the Holy Spirit's means of revealing Jesus Christ is the Word of God. Therefore study the Bible with renewed fervor. After all, Jesus told His disciples a few hours before His death that He would make possible the coming of the Holy Spirit and the writing of the New Testament.

Focusing on the Facts

1. Explain the effect liberal theology has had on the understanding some people have of biblical authority (see p. 46).
2. What do some religious groups add to the revelation of the Bible (see p. 46)?
3. How does the Bible attest to its own interpretation (see pp. 46-47)?
4. How does the teaching of Christ prove that inspiration extends to the precise words of the Bible (Matt. 22:23-33, 41-46; see p. 48)?
5. Why did Christ stop short of a full disclosure of the future to His disciples (John 16:13; see p. 49)?
6. What does "many things" probably refer to in John 16:12 (see p. 49)?
7. What does 2 Peter 1:20-21 tell us about the inspiration of the Old Testament (see p. 50)?
8. Define plenary inspiration (see p. 51).
9. How does the Spirit's guidance to us differ from how He led the disciples (John 16:13; see p. 51)?
10. How do we know that the Holy Spirit will guide us into truth (see p. 52)?
11. What relationship does the Spirit's guidance have with the Word of God (see p. 52)?
12. Explain the connection between the ministry of the Holy Spirit and our knowledge of Christ and the Father (John 16:14-15; 1 Cor. 12:3; see p. 54).

Pondering the Principles

1. The Holy Spirit's ministries of inspiration, illumination, and revelation must be distinguished. Throughout the history of the church, failure to understand the difference among those concepts has caused strife and error. That is one reason you need to know proper principles of interpreting Scripture. Although we no longer receive biblical revelation or inspiration, the Holy Spirit does illumine us. However, illumination will never contradict the Bible. We must always check what we perceive to be the leading of the Holy Spirit against the Word of God. Failure

to do so will inevitably bring disaster. Before you begin reading God's Word, spend a few minutes in prayer, asking God to help you understand its teaching. Consult your local Christian bookstore or library for works that explain how to interpret Scripture correctly. One such work is John MacArthur's Bible Study Guide *How to Study the Bible* (Chicago: Moody, 1985).

2. One test of Spirit-prompted ministry is to ask who is being glorified. It is so easy to exalt oneself under the guise of service to Christ. Even prayer can be perverted, so that the one offering the prayer is lifted up. In Matthew 6:5 Christ says that hypocrites pray "that they may be seen by men." In contrast, the Holy Spirit ministers in such a way that He does not take away Christ's glory. Rather, He is completely consumed with exalting the Lord, not Himself. Religious groups that give greater prominence to the Holy Spirit, a particular minister, or anyone else above Christ are clearly not of God. When you are offered an opportunity to minister, first pause and evaluate your motive. Does that ministry appeal to you because it will allow you to give glory to the Lord? Or are you attracted by the potential for self-glorification?

Scripture Index

Topical Index

Anthropology. *See* Man
Apostles, the
    doctrine of, 51
    inspiration of, 51-53
    selfishness of, 28-29
    unselfishness of, 29-30

Bible, the. *See* Scripture

Calvin, John, sufficiency of
    apostles' doctrine, 51
Christian Science, addition to
    Scripture, 46
Church, the Body of Christ, 17-18
Conscience, the. *See* Conviction
Conviction
    barrier to, 35-36
    conscience and, 41, 43
    Holy Spirit's role in, 35-43
    ignoring, 41, 43
    instruments of, 37-41
    judgment and, 40-41
    object of, 36-37
    righteousness and, 39-40
    sin and, 38-39

Depravity. *See* Man
Disciples, the. *See* Apostles

Eddy, Mary Baker. *See* Christian
    Science
Eschatology, apostolic revelation of, 53
Evangelism
    audience of, 11-12
    content of, 12-13, 15, 19-20,
        42-43
    God's responsibility in, 19
    Holy Spirit's role in. *See*
        Conviction

    legal terminology of, 10
    New Testament, 13
    Old Testament, 13
    pain in, 37
    personal testimony and, 12,
        17-18
    preparing for, 19
    responses to, 10
    Scripture and. *See* content of
    source of, 13-17
    standards for, 12

God, presence of, 9
Gospel, the. *See* Evangelism,
    content of
Guilt. *See* Conviction

Harvey, William, circulatory
    system, 47
Holy Spirit, the
    Christ-centeredness of, 54,
        56. *See also* promise of
    conviction by. *See* Conviction
    filling by, 16-17
    guarantee of. *See* promise of
    illumination by. *See*
        Illumination
    inspiration by. *See* Inspiration
    manifestation of, 17
    ministries of. *See* Conviction,
        Inspiration, Revelation
    power of, 9
    promise of, 8-9, 17, 30
    revelation by. *See* Revelation
    truthfulness of, 51
    witness of. *See* Evangelism

Illumination, inspiration vs.,
    52, 55-56
Inspiration
    apostolic, 52

Holy Spirit's role in, 48-49
illumination vs., 55-56
New Testament, 51
Old Testament, 50
plenary, 51
verbal, 51
Intolerance. *See* Persecution,
    religious

Jehovah's Witnesses, interpre-
    tation of Scripture, 46
Jesus Christ
    Holy Spirit's relation to. *See*
        Holy Spirit
    persecution of, 27-28
    unselfishness of, 30
Judgment, conviction of. *See*
    Conviction

Latter-day Saints. *See*
    Mormonism
Liberal theology, regarding
    Scripture, 46

Man, depravity of, 35-36, 47-48
Ministry. *See* Service
Modalism. *See* Trinity, the
Mormonism, addition to Scrip-
    ture, 46

Neoorthodoxy. *See* Liberal
    theology

Ostracism. *See* Persecution

Paradoxes. *See* Scripture, para-
    doxes in
Paul
    inspiration of, 51-52
    persecution by, 24
Persecution
    description of, 24-26
    facing, 11-12, 19
    inevitability of, 9-10, 22-24

in the name of God. *See*
    religious
modern, 24
ostracism, 25
preparation for, 23
promise of. *See* inevitability of
reason for, 9-10, 25-26
religious, 25-26, 34
Tribulation, 27-28
Prayer, answered, 9

Religion, persecution inspired
    by. *See* Persecution
Revelation
    completion of, 46
    consistency of, 52-53
    content of, 52-54
    Holy Spirit's role in, 50-52
    illumination vs., 55-56
    reason for, 49, 52
    regarding future, 53
Righteousness, conviction of.
    See Conviction
Russell, Charles Taze. *See* Jeho-
    vah's Witnesses
Rutherford, Joseph Franklin.
    See Jehovah's Witnesses

Saul. *See* Paul
Scripture
    addition to, 46
    completion of, 46
    historical accuracy of, 47
    illumination of. *See*
        Illumination
    inspiration of. *See* Inspiration
    interpretation of, 55-56
    Jesus' view of, 48
    liberal view of, 46
    paradoxes in, 47-48
    revelation of. *See* Revelation
    scientific accuracy of, 47
    scope of knowledge, 47
    studying, 54-56

Moody Press, a ministry of the Moody Bible Institute, is designed for education, evangelization, and edification. If we may assist you in knowing more about Christ and the Christian life, please write us without obligation: Moody Press, c/o MLM, Chicago, Illinois 60610.